THE GLOBAL STOCK MARKET CRASH OF 2024 AND ITS LESSONS

How The Fed, A Pandemic, And A War Reshaped The Financial World: The Inside Story Of The Biggest Financial Crisis Since 2008.

Nutshell Nook

All rights reserved. No part of this publication may be reproduced, distributed, or transmitted in any form or by any means, including photocopying, recording, or other electronic or mechanical methods, without the prior written permission of the publisher, except in the case of brief quotations embodied in critical reviews and certain other noncommercial uses permitted by copyright law.

Copyright © Nutshell Nook, 2024

Table of contents

Chapter 1 .... **7**
    The Trigger Point: Unraveling the US Economy........ 7
Chapter 2 .... **18**
    Global Ripple Effects: From Wall Street to Tokyo... 18
Chapter 3 .... **27**
    Sectors in the Crosshairs... 27
Chapter 4 .... **39**
    Historical Perspectives and Future Outlooks.......... 39
Chapter 5 .... **50**
    Lessons for Investors: Strategies in Uncertain Times.
.... 50

Chapter 1

The Trigger Point: Unraveling the US Economy

"In the world of finance, the butterfly effect is not just a theory—it's a daily reality." -Unknown.

On that fateful Monday in August 2024, when dawn dawned over Wall Street, nobody could have foretold the seismic movements that would soon shake the world of finance. The US economy, which has long been seen as the cornerstone of global markets, was beginning to exhibit indications of stress that would soon be felt on other continents. A complicated combination of economic statistics, central bank actions, and the always erratic power of market mood sat at the center of this growing drama.

A few days before, the Federal Reserve, the esteemed organization responsible for guiding the biggest economy globally, had alluded to a forthcoming sequence of reductions in interest rates. Normally, markets would have celebrated such a move as an indication of easier financing and possible economic stimulation. But things were not as they seemed. The market reacted quickly and harshly as traders and analysts started to interpret the Fed's carefully phrased remarks in new ways.

Many saw danger rather than hope in such remarks. The Fed's move to lower interest rates was seen as a reaction rather than a proactive move to maintain growth, acknowledging that the US economy was in trouble and in need of assistance. This view set off a series of sell-offs that quickly engulfed markets spanning from Tokyo to New York.

The Fed's signals did not appear out of thin air. They were presented with a background of mounting economic statistics that had been building for some months. There has been a decreasing trend in manufacturing indicators, indicating a slowdown in industrial output. Orders for durable goods, a crucial measure of consumer and industry confidence, had unexpectedly declined. However, the statistics about employment and payroll raised red flags.

Long seen as a trailing sign of economic health, employment data has started to reveal fissures in the US labor market's foundation. The jobless rate has begun to slowly rise after years of being close to all-time lows. More importantly, there had been a sharp slowdown in the rate of employment growth, with several industries even reporting net losses. Even though these changes were little on their own, when considered in the context of recent economic history, they assumed enormous significance.

Let me introduce you to the Sahm Rule, a very recent yet well-regarded economic indicator. This indicator, named after economist Claudia Sahm, is intended to accurately detect the start of recessions. The national unemployment rate's three-month moving average must increase by 0.5 percentage points or more from its 12-month low for the rule to take effect. The Sahm Rule was flashing red as of August 2024, indicating that the US economy was either in a recession already or was very close to one.

The Sahm Rule's simplicity and effectiveness are its main assets. It had accurately predicted every recession since World War II, often ahead of time compared to more conventional methods. Its signal in the summer of 2024 was especially significant because of the rule's increasing influence on legislators and industry players. A perfect storm of economic worry was produced by the fact that it was raising alarms at the same time as the Fed was hinting at rate reduction.

However, data and indications only provide a portion of the picture. The true drama was playing out in the thoughts and deeds of institutional investors as they struggled with an increasingly unpredictable economic environment. Always a volatile force, investor emotions became the pivot around which markets shook.

Before the August disaster, a tangible uneasiness had descended across boardrooms and trading floors. Economists combed through economic statistics, looking for encouraging signals or validation of their worst suspicions. Fund managers convened for extended strategy meetings, discussing whether to maintain their current positions or relocate to more secure locations. Retail investors found it difficult to interpret the contradicting signals after being inundated with contradicting advice from the financial media.

Perhaps the best way to understand the delicate balance of investor moods is through the lens of game theory. Every actor in the market has to not only evaluate the actual economic facts but also predict how other players will respond. This may create a self-reinforcing cycle of pessimism in an environment of uncertainty. Others are under pressure and sell as some investors do, or else they

10

risk being stuck with depreciating assets. This combination has the power to turn a market decline into a catastrophic event.

An interesting area of research in human behavior is the psychology of market participants during times of crisis. The two main forces behind market movement, greed, and fear, dance intricately together. It was obvious that dread was in control in the moments before the disaster in August 2024. However, investor behavior was motivated by more than simply a fear of losing money. Additionally, there was a worry of losing out on opportunities to profit from what some anticipated would be brief market disruptions or to sell holdings before conditions worsened.

The job of algorithmic trading was to add gasoline to the fire. Recent years have seen a rise in the percentage of market activity driven by computer programs that carry out deals using intricate mathematical models. Even though these algorithms are often commended for increasing market liquidity, in stressful situations, they may also make volatility worse. Many of these systems automatically triggered more sales orders when selling pressure increased, resulting in a feedback loop that magnified market movements.

The interaction between computerized trading systems and human decision-makers increased the level of uncertainty in an already unstable scenario. Certain market watchers contended that the velocity and magnitude of the August fall could alone be accounted for by the impact of these algorithmic traders. Some argued that the market's response was warranted because of the underlying economic issues.

As word of the market turbulence spread, it started to affect actual economic activity, raising the possibility of a recession becoming self-fulfilling. Businesses started to reevaluate employment and investment plans as a result of the sharp decline in their stock values. Customers cut down on their spending because they were concerned about the value of their retirement portfolios and the stability of their employment. Even if each of these responses made sense on its own, taken as a whole, they further lowered expectations for the economy.

Due to the global structure of contemporary finance, issues that started in the US swiftly extended to other markets. Sharp selloffs occurred in European markets, which were already facing economic difficulties, as investors tried to lower the overall risk in their portfolios. The early panic selling was concentrated in Asian markets, whose trading days started after American markets closed.

The Nikkei index for Japan grew to be a particular source of worry. Its worst one-day performance since the peak of the COVID-19 epidemic was the 12% decline it suffered. The "yen carry trade," a well-liked tactic among foreign investors that involves borrowing low-yielding yen to invest in higher-yielding assets abroad, was winding down, which made this abrupt swing even more startling. The rush by market players to unwind these bets put further selling pressure on Japanese equities and increased demand for the yen, which further complicated the state of the world economy.

The role of central banks in this developing crisis came up for much discussion. The Federal Reserve was now in a difficult situation after announcing its plan to lower interest rates. Should it carry out such measures to keep the economy and markets stable? Or would doing so be seen as a confession of more serious issues, which would make the fear worse? Both the European Central Bank and the Bank of Japan were in comparable situations, knowing full well that investors worldwide would be closely watching their moves.

As the crisis worsened, the focus shifted to its wider economic ramifications. Despite its significance, the economy is not the stock market. Sharp market declines, however, may have important consequences in the real world. During market collapses, the wealth effect—the propensity for people to spend more when their perceived wealth increases—functions in reverse. People often cut back on their spending when they see a fall in the value of their investment portfolios, which may cause the economy to collapse.

Furthermore, the stock market serves as a major source of funding for numerous businesses. A protracted recession may increase the cost and difficulty of raising capital for businesses, which may discourage investment and impede economic expansion. For IT businesses, which had recently been the engine of economic expansion, this dynamic was especially alarming. The IT industry's ability to drive innovation and job creation has come under scrutiny in light of the recent dramatic decrease in its stocks.

Economic disparity was also a topic of considerable interest after the market crisis in August 2024. Although stock market volatility directly affects investors, it also has repercussions for the general public, often in unequal ways. Employees in retail and manufacturing—two sectors vulnerable to economic fluctuations—were more likely to experience layoffs. Those who had substantial stock holdings, on the other hand, saw their paper riches disappear, which could have delayed retirement or changed long-term financial goals.

Economists and politicians were obliged to address basic issues about the structure of contemporary capitalism as they struggled to deal with the crisis that was developing. Had unrealistic expectations been raised by the protracted bull market of the years before? Were the conventional instruments of monetary policy enough to handle the many problems of an international, technologically advanced economy? Furthermore, how may the advantages of economic expansion be dispersed more fairly to build a stronger system?

The catastrophe of August 2024 also brought attention to how intertwined the world's markets are becoming. Financial contagion may spread at an astounding rate in this day of immediate communication and round-the-clock trade. Things that used to be confined behind national boundaries may now cause panic throughout the globe. Because they must coordinate their actions across jurisdictions and time zones, regulators and policymakers face considerable hurdles as a result of this fact.

With the initial market collapse having passed, speculation over whether this was a short-term correction or the start of a longer-term decline started to gain traction. It was natural to make historical analogies; some saw similarities to the Black Monday fall of 1987, while others saw links to the financial crisis of 2008. However, since each financial crisis is different, it is influenced by the social, technical, and economic circumstances of its time.

The August 2024 collapse happened in the context of growing geopolitical tensions, changing population patterns, and major technological advancements. The global financial system has become more complicated as a result of the emergence of cryptocurrencies and decentralized finance. The link between climate change and economic risk is becoming more widely acknowledged. Additionally, the aging populations of many wealthy nations were altering their investing and saving habits.

In this particular context, the US economy's collapse and the ensuing market turbulence were indications of more profound structural shifts than just financial occurrences. They compelled an examination of the underlying presumptions of contemporary economic theory and practice. One thing became evident as investors, politicians, and people alike struggled to understand the ramifications of these events: a new and unpredictable economic age was dawning, one that would call for audacious thinking and daring solutions to overcome the obstacles that lay ahead.

Chapter 2

Global Ripple Effects: From Wall Street to Tokyo

"When America sneezes, the world catches a cold." - Klemens von Metternich (adapted)

Because of the long-standing interdependence of the world's financial systems, shocks from one large country may send shockwaves across other big economies. This economic interdependence was brought home sharply by the events of August 2024, which started as Wall Street tremors and swiftly turned into a global financial earthquake. This chapter explores the complicated network of responses from the world's markets, focusing in particular on the seismic changes that were seen in Japan and the intricate dynamics surrounding the country's currency.

The greatest economy in the world and a barometer of the state of the global financial system, the United States, was the source of the first indications of problems. Concerns about an impending recession in the United States prompted investors all over the globe to reevaluate their holdings. A major barometer of the strength of the US stock market, the S&P 500, fell 3% in a single trading session, while the tech-heavy Nasdaq fell 3.43%. Despite their importance, these numbers simply alluded to the global pandemonium that was about to break out.

Asian markets were the first to experience the full impact of the tsunami as word of the U.S. market decline spread. Due to the interdependence of world finance, traders in Shanghai, Hong Kong, and Tokyo were already quite cautious as their trading day got underway. As a consequence, there was a sudden and intense selling wave that was sparked by a combination of anxiety and algorithmic trading systems that were meant to react to market volatility.

With losses over 8%, the Hang Seng Index in Hong Kong had its biggest one-day plunge in more than ten years. Little improvement was seen in the Chinese mainland markets, as the Shanghai Composite and Shenzhen Component both had declines of more than 6%. Throughout the trading day, the quick sell-off repeatedly set off circuit breakers, briefly stopping trades to stop panic selling. Nevertheless, when investors rushed to sell their holdings and shift to what they believed to be safe-haven assets, these steps proved to be mostly ineffectual.

Over $100 billion in market value vanished from the Australian Securities Exchange (ASX) in a couple of hours. The extent of the casualties underscored the gravity of the present problem and was reminiscent of the early stages of the COVID-19 epidemic. A worldwide recession prompted worries about the demand for raw materials in the future, which notably hurt resource equities, which had been rising sharply on the back of the commodities boom.

Panicked scenes emerged in European markets as the selling tsunami swept westward. Every sector saw severe losses as the STOXX 600 index for all of Europe fell by more than 5%. The DAX in Germany, the CAC 40 in France, and the FTSE 100 in the UK all had losses of more than 4%. Many investors were taken aback by the depth and speed of the fall, which resulted in a shortage of liquidity as purchasers left the market.

Still, the most dramatic moments took place in Japan. Japan's main stock index, the Nikkei 225, fell by an extraordinary 12% in a single trading day. This fall surpassed even the notorious Black Monday crash of 1987 and the chaos that followed the Fukushima tragedy in 2011 as the greatest one-day percentage decline in the index's history.

The Nikkei's disproportionate response has many causes. Because of its export-driven economy, Japan is especially vulnerable to changes in the world economy, particularly those that come from the US, which is its main trade partner. Investors immediately estimated the possible effect on Japanese exporters, including electronics firms like Sony and Panasonic as well as major automakers like Toyota and Honda, as concerns about a U.S. recession increased.

In addition, the Japanese market had been experiencing great success in the months before the crisis due to hopes for the nation's economic recovery and corporate governance changes. This rendered it especially susceptible to an abrupt change in opinion. The quick unwinding of long positions made the sell-off worse and led to a downward spiral in prices and a self-reinforcing cycle of liquidation.

As the crisis deepened, the Bank of Japan (BOJ) found itself in a vulnerable situation. The BOJ has been implementing a very loose monetary policy, which included negative interest rates and large asset purchases, for years, in contrast to its counterparts in other industrialized countries. As a result, it had few traditional measures at its disposal to quell market turbulence. While selling pressure persisted unabatedly, emergency announcements from BOJ officials promising to preserve stability had little immediate effect.

The unwinding of the yen carry trade, a well-liked tactic among international investors that had major ramifications for the Japanese stock market as well as the larger currency markets, added gasoline to the fire. In the yen carry trade, the low-yielding yen is borrowed and invested in foreign assets with higher yields, usually denominated in dollars. Because of Japan's very low interest rates and the relatively stable value of the yen, this method has been successful for many years.

Nevertheless, investors scrambled to unwind their holdings as global risk aversion surged. As traders cashed out of their short positions, this resulted in a spike in demand for the yen, which quickly strengthened the Japanese currency relative to other major currencies. Though usually seen as a sign of the desire for safe havens, the yen's gain presented more difficulties for Japanese exporters already suffering from the fall of the stock market.

There were significant ramifications for countries outside of Japan from the dissolution of the yen carry trade. The selling off of holdings in assets and currencies with greater yields by investors has a cascading impact on developing economies. Currencies that had profited from carry trade inflows, such as the Australian dollar, South African rand, and Brazilian real, saw severe depreciation. The already turbulent global financial environment became even more complicated as a result of this currency volatility.

The perceived safety of the world's reserve currency led investors to first seek out and boost the U.S. dollar in the foreign exchange markets. But when rumors spread that the Federal Reserve would have to slash interest rates significantly to prevent a recession, this tendency swiftly turned around. As substitute safe-havens, the euro and Swiss franc gained value relative to a basket of major world currencies.

The cryptocurrency market, which supporters often cited as a buffer against volatility in the regular financial markets, turned out to be just as vulnerable to the worldwide sell-off. The value of Bitcoin, the biggest cryptocurrency by market capitalization, fell by more than 20% in a single day. This fall cast doubt on the idea that cryptocurrencies are "digital gold" and showed how they continue to be correlated with riskier assets in times of severe market stress.

As the crisis worsened, the focus shifted to the possibility of financial system contagion. Margin-called positions were strained by the rapid changes in price and the heightened volatility, which had a ripple effect in the banking industry. There have been reports of substantial losses at many big hedge funds, which has sparked worries about possible defaults and the effects they might have on prime brokers and the larger financial system.

Global central banks frantically moved to address the growing catastrophe. The Bank of England made hints about the potential to revive previously discontinued quantitative easing measures, while the European Central Bank called an emergency conference to consider such actions. But in the face of such broad market fear, these policies' efficacy remained questionable.

The global unrest did not spare the commodities markets. Fears of declining global demand caused oil prices to collapse, with benchmark crude oil futures plummeting by more than 10%. This drop increased worries about deflation in major economies and had direct effects on countries that produce energy. Increased demand was seen for gold, an asset long viewed as a haven, but its gains were limited by the strength of the yen and the need for some investors to sell their holdings to satisfy margin calls in other markets.

A growing number of doubts about the structural stability of the global financial system surfaced as trading rooms from New York to London to Singapore struggled with the impending crisis. There have been requests for a review of circuit breakers and other market stability devices due to the rapid and severe changes in the market. Authorities were questioned about how well-prepared they were for a market event of this magnitude, especially considering the growing importance of high-frequency trading and passive investing techniques in the last several years.

As the days passed, it became more and more clear how many people had been affected by the market collapse. Accounts of mental health issues and trader burnout were common, underscoring the extreme strain experienced by people working in the financial markets. Investment banks mandated staff leisure breaks, while hedge funds had to deal with distressed investors' redemption demands.

The historical collapse of the Nikkei had a significant psychological effect on Japan. After the asset price bubble burst in the early 1990s, the nation had endured decades of economic stagnation; hence, the recent market gains were seen as an indication of the economy's resurgence. The abrupt turn of events prompted reflection on the sustainability of Japan's economic model and its susceptibility to outside shocks among the public and politicians alike.

When the initial market shock started to fade, the focus shifted to the crisis's longer-term effects. Concerns over the direction of globalization and the interdependence of financial markets surfaced. While some pundits advocated for a return to more regionally focused economic models, others said that the crisis proved the need for more robust international financial cooperation and regulation.

The events of August 2024 provided a sobering reminder of the interconnectedness of the globe and the vulnerability of the global financial system. The effects of this market collapse would be felt for years to come, changing public views of the financial markets, investing techniques, and policy approaches from the trading floors of Wall Street to Tokyo's neon-lit streets.

Chapter 3

Sectors in the Crosshairs

"The stock market is a device for transferring money from the impatient to the patient." - Warren Buffett

Some industries found themselves right in the line of fire for frightened investors in August 2024, as the world markets reeled from the shock of possible US recession worries. The IT sector, which was previously seen as a bulwark of expansion and innovation, seemed exposed. Bonds and other safe-haven investments saw a spike in demand. In the meantime, concerns were raised by changes in consumer purchasing habits in the retail industry. This chapter explores these important areas, looking at how they performed throughout the market volatility and what their results could mean for the overall economy.

Thanks to advances in semiconductors, cloud computing, and artificial intelligence, the technology industry has been booming for years. Businesses like Nvidia, whose stock values reached stratospheric heights, had turned into the tech boom's poster children. Investors flooded these businesses with cash, placing their bets on ongoing innovation and market leadership. But when market anxiety about a recession set in, tech equities seemed expensive and dangerous.

The stock of Nvidia, which had spearheaded the AI revolution, fell by as much as 15% in a single day. This sharp decline brought to light how susceptible even the most prosperous IT companies are to general economic worries. The company's success had been strongly correlated with the AI boom, as its graphics processing units (GPUs) were becoming essential parts of data centers and machine learning applications. The exorbitant valuation of Nvidia came under criticism as investors reevaluated the short-term growth prospects of AI in a possibly recessionary climate.

Not that other massive IT companies were exempt. The stock prices of Apple, Microsoft, Amazon, and Alphabet, the parent company of Google, all saw large declines. Known as the "Big Tech" or "FAANG" stocks together, these businesses have recently played a significant role in determining the success of the market as a whole. Their fall had a disproportionate effect on market indexes such as the Nasdaq and the S&P 500 due to their outsized influence.

Concerns over the sustainability of the tech sector's growth trajectory were raised by the sell-off in equities.

Critics said that hype and conjecture had replaced the need for appraisals to be based on actual business performance. Drawing parallels with the dot-com boom of the late 1990s, they cautioned that a costly correction was long coming.

However, proponents of the IT industry claimed that the fundamental developments propelling expansion—digital transformation, cloud adoption, and AI integration—remained unaltered. They did not see a fundamental change in the industry's prospects but rather saw the market decline as a brief setback. Strong IT businesses with sound financials and tested business strategies, according to these experts, will weather the storm and come out stronger.

An important segment of the IT sector, the semiconductor industry, has its own set of difficulties. Even before the market collapse, chip makers were battling supply chain problems and geopolitical unrest. Their perspective became even more difficult in light of the recessionary danger. The amount that consumers and businesses spend on infrastructure and electronic devices is directly correlated with the demand for semiconductors. A downturn in the economy may result in fewer orders from big chip customers, such as automobile manufacturers and smartphone makers.

Despite these challenges, several industry watchers anticipated success for semiconductor companies. Growth prospects may arise from the desire for more chip production capacity in the US and Europe, which is being fueled by worries over supply chain resilience. Furthermore, it was anticipated that the demand for certain chip types would be sustained by the ongoing development of 5G networks and the growing use of Internet of Things (IoT) devices.

Investors sought solace in conventional safe-haven assets as tech stocks collapsed, with government bonds emerging as a popular alternative. The flight to bonds was a reflection of a more general change in market players' appetite for risk, as they placed more value on capital preservation than possible returns. The yield curve was inverted as a result of the increase in demand for bonds, which is sometimes seen as a sign of an impending recession.

Particularly robust inflows were seen in the U.S. Treasury market, which is regarded as the safest and most liquid bond market globally. Bond prices increased, leading to a dramatic decline in yields on 10-year Treasury notes, which are inversely correlated with prices. There were significant ramifications for the bond market outside of this yield decline. Reduced long-term interest rates have an impact on business borrowing costs as well as mortgage rates, which may have an impact on economic activity in several different sectors.

The rush for bonds extended beyond US Treasury securities. Strong demand was also seen for German bonds, Japanese government bonds (JGBs), and other national debt that was seen as a haven. This worldwide occurrence highlighted how intertwined financial markets are and how pervasive recession concerns are.

The flight to safety helped corporate bonds as well, especially those issued by businesses with good credit ratings. Investors looking for better returns than government bonds while keeping a relatively low-risk profile poured money into investment-grade corporate paper. On the other hand, the situation with high-yield or "junk" bonds was less clear. The greater rates on offer drew some investors in, but others were concerned about the heightened default risk these instruments carried in a recessionary climate.

The way the bond market behaved at this time of extreme market volatility reminded us of how important it is to the financial system. Bond yields serve as crucial economic indicators, affecting monetary policy choices and forming expectations about future economic circumstances, in addition to offering investors a haven.

The abrupt increase in bond prices and subsequent decline in rates, however, also sparked worries about possible market distortions. A few experts cautioned that the rush into bonds may burst the market, with prices influenced more by underlying economic fundamentals than by investor concern. They issued a warning, stating that if interest rates were to increase suddenly, investors who piled into bonds at historically low yields may suffer large losses.

During this time, central banks' involvement in the bond market came under closer examination. Initially unsettling stock investors, the Federal Reserve's hinting at a possible rate reduction had a more nuanced effect on the bond market. Lower policy rates tend to boost bond prices, but they also signal worries about the expansion of the economy. Every comment made by Fed officials was extensively examined by market players, who sought to determine how the central bank would react in terms of policy and how serious the recession risks were.

Important clues about the state of the actual economy came from changes in consumer spending habits as investors struggled with developments in the financial markets. The online furniture and home goods store Wayfair issued a warning, which served as a sobering reminder of the possible effects of a recession on customer behavior.

Retailers were shocked to see that Wayfair's client spending had decreased by about 25% from its high levels three years before. The CEO of the firm, Niraj Shah, highlighted the severity of the slowdown by drawing comparisons between the present downturn and the contraction that occurred during the Great Financial Crisis.

Wayfair made a statement that was especially important considering its standing in the e-commerce industry. Wayfair, an online-only company, was thought to be relatively immune to the difficulties faced by physical storefronts. Because of its emphasis on home furnishings, which are usually seen as discretionary expenditures, it served as a helpful gauge of consumer confidence and willingness to spend money on non-essentials.

Wayfair's warning has far-reaching consequences that go far beyond the firm. It sparked concerns about the overall well-being of the e-commerce industry, which had grown quickly in previous years—especially during the COVID-19 epidemic. If internet merchants were having trouble, it meant that shoppers were cutting down on their expenditures anywhere they could.

Investors and analysts rapidly began to scrutinize other stores, searching for indications of similar tendencies. Businesses in the fashion, electronics, and home improvement industries were under more pressure to provide information on their sales projections. The back-to-school shopping season, which is usually a profitable time for stores, has drawn attention as a possible gauge of consumer mood.

The change in consumer buying habits brought to light the intricate relationship that exists between retail success, consumer psychology, and economic situations. A canary in the coal mine indicating a wider consumer slump, several experts contended that Wayfair's warning was just a normal adjustment after the pandemic-induced spike in home-related purchases.

Companies that produce luxury items, which are sometimes thought to be immune to economic downturns because of their affluent clientele, also seemed to be under stress. Concerns over the impending slowdown's global character were heightened by reports of declining demand in important countries like China. The success of luxury brands started to be extensively observed as a gauge of the robustness of discretionary spending and the confidence of upper-class consumers.

Conversely, there was a rise in investor interest in dollar shops and cheap merchants. Viewed as possible defensive bets in a recessionary context, these firms often do well during economic downturns when customers trade down to cheaper alternatives. Another piece of information for those attempting to predict the direction of consumer spending was their stock performance in comparison to higher-end shops.

Pressure also mounted on the car industry, which accounted for a sizable portion of expenditure on consumer durables. The switch to electric cars and problems with the supply chain had long been plaguing automakers. Their perspective became even more difficult in light of the recessionary danger. Auto sales data became one of the most widely followed metrics, with any indication of declining demand being seen as being indicative of more serious economic issues.

The effects of shifting customer behavior were seen in services as well as conventional retail. Rekindled uncertainty confronted the tourism and hotel sectors, which had been recovering rapidly from the pandemic-induced downturn. We looked closely at airplane, hotel, and vacation package booking trends to look for indications that customers were cutting down on discretionary travel expenditures.

Several important problems plagued analysts and investors as they tried to make sense of these changing consumer behaviors. Was the spending slowdown just a transitory phenomenon brought on, for example, by worries about inflation? Or did it point to a more fundamental change in consumer behavior, maybe a reflection of underlying concerns about the direction of the economy?

The responses to these queries have significant effects on the whole economy as well as the retail industry. In industrialized economies such as the US, consumer expenditure usually makes up a sizable share of GDP. A persistent decline in consumer spending can have repercussions for many different businesses, which might make recessionary predictions come true.

While they prepared their responses to the economic issues, policymakers, and central bankers kept a careful eye on these developments in consumer spending. Policy talks began to center on how consumer confidence, spending habits, and the state of the economy as a whole interact. There were heated discussions about how to strike the right balance between reducing inflationary pressures via tighter monetary policy and boosting consumer expenditure through stimulus programs.

The divergent fates of various industries throughout the market upheaval brought attention to how difficult and sometimes unanticipated economic transformations can be. The tech equities that were once considered unstoppable growth engines now seemed susceptible to worries of a recession and changing investor attitudes. Previously disregarded in bull markets, bonds gained prominence as investors sought security. In the meantime, shifts in consumer buying habits offered significant new information on the state of the actual economy, with far-reaching consequences for the retail industry.

These industry-specific trends served as a helpful reminder that not all segments of the market are always equally impacted by economic shifts. Certain industries prospered, while others experienced growth or stability. It was a struggle for investors, analysts, and policymakers to separate the movements that reflected more fundamental changes in the economic environment from those that were just short-term responses to market anxiety.

Chapter 4

Historical Perspectives and Future Outlooks

History doesn't repeat itself, but it often rhymes." - Mark Twain

Following the stock market crisis of 2024, investors and economists struggled to make sense of the chaos that shook the world's financial institutions. We need to have a historical perspective on this occurrence by comparing it to other market crises. We may more accurately predict possible recovery routes and assess the impact of political considerations on economic results by comprehending these historical analogies.

The abrupt and dramatic market decline of 2024 is eerily reminiscent of several previous market crises, each with its own distinct features and lessons. The Great Depression was announced by the 1929 Wall Street Crash, which serves as a sobering warning of the disastrous outcomes that may result from market euphoria. Because of cheap borrowing and rampant speculation, stock values had risen to unaffordable heights before 1929. After the bubble broke, there was a protracted period of severe unemployment, company closures, and bank failures.

The Great Depression and the crisis of 2024 are not as severe as they were, but they do have some similarities. Periods of economic optimism and rapid market expansion, especially in the technology sector, preceded both disasters. The excitement around new technologies such as radio and cars in the 1920s is reflected in the emergence of artificial intelligence and its potential to bring about revolutionary change. But since the 1930s, economic safety nets and regulations have helped avert a full-blown economic collapse comparable to the Great Depression.

The 1987 Black Monday disaster, in which the Dow Jones Industrial Average fell by 22.6% in a single day, is another pertinent contrast. Computerized trading algorithms were mostly blamed for this incident, as they increased selling pressure and set off a vicious cycle of declining prices and panic selling. Similar technical reasons have affected the crisis of 2024; however, it was not as abrupt. Market fluctuations have been exacerbated by high-frequency trading algorithms and the interconnectivity of global markets, resulting in fast sell-offs across numerous asset classes and nations.

Another interesting similarity is the dot-com bubble crash in 2000. Similar to the tech-driven bubble that preceded the crisis of 2024, excitement about the developing internet economy in the late 1990s led to a spike in the value of technology stocks. The market corrected severely and for a long time when inflated expectations were not met by reality. The aftermath of the dot-com bust offers important insights into how overpriced industries may go through difficult but necessary corrections, which eventually result in longer-term, more sustainable development.

Possibly the most current and pertinent analogy is the Global Financial Crisis of 2008. This crisis brought to light the interdependence of the world's financial systems and the perils of intricate, opaque financial products. It was sparked by the collapse of the US housing market and the subsequent bankruptcy of significant banking institutions. The worldwide scope and quick spread across markets of the crisis in 2024 are some of its commonalities. The underlying reasons, however, are quite different: systemic flaws in the financial industry are less likely to be the primary cause of the 2024 recession than worries about monetary policy and economic fundamentals.

While these historical parallels provide insightful background for comprehending the crisis of 2024, they also highlight the distinctive features of every market event. In 2024, the world economy will be more integrated than ever, thanks to immediate information sharing and very advanced financial tools. Both positive and negative market movements may be amplified by this interconnection, which might result in more frequent and severe volatility.

Several prospective triggers that might aid in stabilizing markets and rekindling economic development are becoming apparent as we move toward recovery. Just like in previous crises, the activities of central banks will be critical. Although the Federal Reserve's hinting at interest rate decreases first alarmed the markets, if wisely executed, they may eventually act as a cushion for the economy. However, considering that many industrialized countries already have low interest rates, the ability of monetary policy to stimulate development may be restricted.

Measures of fiscal policy may prove to be effective instruments for economic recovery. Spending by the government on social programs, R&D, and infrastructure may create long-term economic competitiveness while simultaneously acting as an instant boost. The difficulty is striking a balance between immediate stimulation and long-term budgetary sustainability, which is a difficult task that decision-makers must carefully evaluate.

Although it is a cause of market instability, technological innovation may also be a driver of recovery. Technological developments in biotechnology, renewable energy, and artificial intelligence might lead to the emergence of new sectors, increased productivity, and economic expansion. But to fully reap these rewards, disruptive elements of technological progress, such as possible job displacement, and growing inequality, must be carefully managed.

The dynamics of global commerce will have a big impact on how the recovery progresses. Modern supply systems are interdependent, so economic recovery cannot happen in a vacuum. A faster global economic recovery may result from initiatives to lower trade barriers, settle pending conflicts, and promote international collaboration. On the other hand, a shift toward economic nationalism and protectionism can exacerbate the slump and reduce development opportunities.

Resolving global tensions may also act as a stimulant for the market to rebound. Market volatility and economic uncertainty have been exacerbated by ongoing wars and trade disputes. Any advancement in these problems' resolution might increase investor confidence and spur the economy. However, since international relations are complicated, these decisions are often erratic and cumbersome.

We must recognize the importance of market psychology as we contemplate the path to recovery. Market fluctuations may sometimes be strongly influenced by investor attitudes, even when they are not influenced by underlying economic facts. A long-term recovery will depend on the markets and the economy as a whole being trusted again. Policymakers and corporate leaders' good communication techniques may be combined with real economic advances in this process.

It is important to consider the possibility of fundamental economic changes as a boost to the economy and future growth. Crises often highlight the flaws in economic systems and provide chances for significant change. In the long term, addressing problems like corporate governance, environmental sustainability, and income inequality may result in a more robust and just economic system.

Since we're talking about political issues, the US election that is coming up soon might have a significant impact on market mood and economic policies. Financial markets have always been significantly impacted by presidential elections, both before election day and after the results are announced. The nation's economic problems and the opposing political ideologies of the main contenders make the 2024 election especially important.

An important factor for both investors and economists to consider is how the election will affect fiscal policy. Approaches to government spending, taxes, and deficit management may differ across regimes. A move toward more expansionary fiscal policies may provide market confidence and economic growth with a temporary boost. However, these advantageous benefits could be mitigated by worries about long-term budgetary sustainability.

Another area where the result of the election might have a significant impact on the financial markets and the economy is regulatory policy. Regulations that impact industries like energy, healthcare, and technology might change, changing the dynamics of the market and how investments are made. The way antitrust laws are enforced, especially for big tech businesses, may have a significant impact on market structure and company values.

With its effects on international economic connections, trade policy is probably going to be a major topic of discussion throughout the election. Market players will be keenly observing the next administration's position on current trade deals, tariffs, and economic connections with important allies like China. Any substantial change in trade policy may cause global supply networks to realign and affect the competitiveness of different sectors.

Even if it is indirect, the election's impact on monetary policy is nonetheless significant. Even though the Federal Reserve is an autonomous institution, its decision-making process may be impacted by political developments. Subject to political approval, the choice of the chairman and governors of the Federal Reserve may influence the long-term course of monetary policy. Market players will be watching for any indications of possible changes in the Fed's mission or membership.

Economic factors are becoming more and more entwined with environmental and climatic policy. The results of the election might have a big impact on how green energy projects, carbon pricing schemes, and environmental policies develop. These regulations may provide obstacles for certain companies, especially those involved in the fossil fuel industry, but they can also open up new economic possibilities.

The election has an influence on foreign relations in addition to domestic policy. The US's attitude on topics like climate change, involvement in international organizations, and approach to global economic governance may all have an impact on the global economy. The results of the election might have an impact on global development prospects and market stability by influencing international collaboration on economic concerns.

It is important to acknowledge that there is a bidirectional link between politics and the economy. Voter attitude and, ultimately, the result of the election will undoubtedly be influenced by the economic circumstances before the election. This feedback cycle makes projecting the election's economic effects much more difficult.

We must have an impartial viewpoint when we examine these political aspects. Even though elections may have a big short-term effect on the direction of policy and market mood, many other variables affect the economy's long-term trajectory more than any one political event. Regardless of the results of the election, global economic trends, demographic changes, and technological advancements will continue to influence the economic environment.

It is a complicated mix of historical precedents, recovery drivers, and political issues that investors and corporate leaders must negotiate. While market downturns may be severe and disruptive, there is evidence from previous crises that they can also provide possibilities for innovation, reform, and fresh prosperity. The secret is to keep an eye on the big picture while being flexible enough to adjust to quickly shifting economic conditions.

The road to recovery from the 2024 crisis will not be straightforward or predictable. Global events, governmental choices, technical developments, and economic fundamentals will all continue to interact to complexly impact market dynamics. Stakeholders may better position themselves to weather economic storms and seize new opportunities by comprehending the significance of political issues, recognizing possible growth accelerators, and learning from historical views.

Similar to its predecessors, the stock market crisis of 2024 is expected to be regarded as a turning point in economic history. Its final effects will be determined not just by the market's immediate reactions and legislative responses but also by the longer-term shifts in corporate practices, regulatory frameworks, and economic theory that it inspires. The lessons of the past and the potential of the future provide both caution and optimism for the global economic landscape as we navigate these unknown seas.

Chapter 5

Lessons for Investors: Strategies in Uncertain Times.

"The stock market is a device for transferring money from the impatient to the patient." - Warren Buffett

Following the stock market crisis of 2024, investors throughout the globe were faced with never-before-seen levels of volatility and uncertainty. The once fairly predictable global economic scene has evolved into a complicated web of interrelated possibilities and hazards. Following what many labeled "The Great Unraveling," the investing community was confronted with a sobering realization: the game had shifted and adaptability was now essential to survive rather than discretionary.

There has never been a more important or difficult time to master the skill of reading economic tea leaves. Separating signal from noise has become a highly valued talent at a time when information travels at the speed of light and algorithms may cause enormous market moves in a matter of microseconds. Investors who used to rely only on conventional economic indicators now had to comb through a dizzying number of data sets, such as sentiment research from social media and satellite images of large shops' parking lots.

Take Maria Chen, a seasoned fund manager with more than 20 years of expertise, as an example. Chen observed little change in consumer behavior in the months before the 2024 collapse, which contrasted with the optimistic outlook provided by government economic projections. Her methods included monitoring real-time data on mobile payments, examining foot traffic patterns in key city retail centers, and detecting a slowdown in discretionary spending well in advance of quarterly earnings announcements. She was able to limit losses and modify her portfolio due to her foresight when the market eventually caught up with the actual situation.

However, interpreting the economic tea leaves involves more than simply identifying impending downturns. Finding chances that others may overlook is as vital. Consider the renewable energy industry in the context of the 2024 financial crisis. Amidst the economic turmoil, investors sought refuge in conventional safe havens such as government bonds and gold. However, those who kept

50

a close eye on global policy trends and technical improvements realized that the shift toward green energy would probably happen more quickly. These astute investors set themselves up for big returns in the years that followed by making investments in carefully chosen businesses in front of this shift.

It is impossible to overestimate the value of diversity in a market prone to volatility, but the events of 2024 exposed that a lot of investors were misinformed about what real diversification meant. Due to the interdependence of world markets, assets that had previously shown little correlation began to move in unison, exposing several ostensibly "balanced" portfolios to large losses.

Financial expert James Kwesi, who is located in Accra, Ghana, discovered this the hard way. Kwesi had urged his customers to diversify across several asset classes and geographical areas before the crisis, thinking that this strategy would provide sufficient protection against market turbulence. But he watched in horror as stocks, bonds, and even alternative assets like real estate investment trusts crashed at the same time due to worries of a US recession that sparked a worldwide sell-off.

Following this, Kwesi set out to reinterpret diversification in light of contemporary circumstances. He started adding investments to his customers' portfolios that had distinct risk profiles and return objectives. This comprised investments in private markets, which provided some protection from the daily volatility of public exchanges, and allocations to trend-following techniques, which may benefit from prolonged market swings in either direction.

Furthermore, Kwesi understood the need for dynamic diversification, which modifies portfolio allocations in response to shifting correlation patterns and market circumstances. To develop more robust investing strategies that may withstand future storms, he periodically stress-tested portfolios under different economic scenarios and used advanced risk management methods.

Beyond asset allocation, diversification was also an idea. Astute investors understood the value of broadening their sources of information and using analytical techniques. They looked for unconventional ideas, conversed with specialists from many fields, and used artificial intelligence to analyze enormous volumes of data and find connections between economic factors that weren't immediately apparent.

The hardest thing about investing during times of tremendous volatility is trying to have a long-term perspective while the market is reacting in the short term. Because the human brain is designed to react quickly to danger, it is all too easy to give in to panic selling or rash decisions during a market meltdown.

A researcher in behavioral finance at the National University of Singapore, Dr. Sarah Lim, studied how investors behaved during the crisis of 2024. Her research showed a clear disparity between institutional investors with long-term mandates and ordinary investors. Pension funds and endowments with multi-decade investment horizons took advantage of the market slump to purchase premium assets at lower prices, while many individual investors liquidated their holdings at or around the bottom of the market, locking in significant losses.

According to Dr. Lim's study, it is crucial to have a clear investing philosophy and to adhere to it, particularly when the market is stressed. She discovered that investors were far less likely to make emotionally charged choices that jeopardized their financial security if they had made the effort to clearly define their long-term objectives and risk tolerance before the crisis.

The collapse of the market in 2024 also highlighted the significance of regular portfolio rebalancing, which compels investors to sell assets that have become too expensive and purchase those that have grown too cheap. This methodical approach fosters a contrarian attitude that may be quite helpful during market extremes, in addition to helping to preserve the intended risk profile.

However, having a long-term perspective does not entail ignoring immediate dangers. Investors who were able to combine tactical flexibility with strategic patience were the most successful both during and after the crisis. They were prepared to make moderate modifications in reaction to shifting economic circumstances, but they stayed true to their underlying investing theses.

Consider the Tanaka family office in Osaka, which amassed its fortune over many generations by making cautious, long-term investments in both domestic and foreign markets. The family office's investment committee called an emergency meeting during the 2024 crisis when the Nikkei fell 12% in a single day. Rather than becomingthan alarmed, they went back over their investment policy statement and came to the same basic conclusions regarding the prospects for the long-term development of their key assets.

Equipped with this confidence, the Tanaka family office increased its ownership in high-conviction holdings by investing new funds in addition to holding onto its current assets. They saw that the price and fundamental worth had been disconnected due to the market's short-term response, offering a unique chance to purchase good companies at fire-sale rates.

However, the family office did not follow a "buy and hold" approach mindlessly. To determine if their portfolio firms could withstand the current economic storm, they carried out in-depth examinations of them. They had to make the painful choice to stop losing money and reallocate it to more viable chances when they saw systemic flaws or insurmountable obstacles.

The need to keep dry powder, or cash reserves that may be strategically used amid market disruptions, was further brought home by the crisis of 2024. A fortunate group of investors, who had enough cash going into the crisis, were able to profit from widespread mispricing, while others were compelled to sell their assets at negative prices.

A new breed of investor emerged as the dust settled and markets started their gradual recovery. This investor understood that success in the post-2024 world necessitated a careful balancing act between qualitative and quantitative judgment, short-term nimbleness and long-term vision, global awareness and local insight.

These investors realized that although economic models and historical data were still useful resources, they were insufficient on their own. The intricacy of contemporary financial markets necessitated a more comprehensive strategy that integrated knowledge from a wide range of disciplines, including psychology, geopolitics, and climate science.

The crisis also acted as a potent reminder that financial markets are an integral part of society as a whole. Those investors that closely monitored social and environmental aspects prospered in its aftermath, understanding that sustainable business practices and good social effect are crucial to long-term wealth development.

The investing world as a whole still remembers the hard-learned lessons from the 2024 market crash, which included shattered expectations and monetary losses. However, these lessons offered a basis for developing more solid, durable, and ultimately profitable investing strategies for individuals who were prepared to change and develop.

One thing became evident as markets kept shifting and new difficulties arose: in the dynamic world of investment, the capacity to learn, unlearn, and relearn would be the ultimate competitive edge. By adopting this perspective, those who turned market turbulence into a source of opportunity positioned themselves not merely to weather future crises but to prosper in the face of uncertainty.

Investing in uncertain times is not a voyage for the weak of heart. It requires emotional control, intellectual curiosity, and a steadfast dedication to ongoing development. However, there may be significant financial and personal advantages for those who are ready to go on this adventure. Beyond just increasing their money, investors get a greater grasp of the world and their position in it by navigating the intricacies of today's markets.

The lessons learned from the 2024 financial crisis will continue to influence investing tactics going forward. In an increasingly uncertain environment, the investors who absorb these lessons—who learn to diversify with sophistication, read the economic tea leaves with discernment, and strike a balance between short-term flexibility and long-term vision—will be the most likely to achieve long-term success.

The fact that there is no ultimate lesson is maybe the most significant lesson of all. In the ever-evolving world of investment, what is wise today could be foolish tomorrow. The people who maintain their humility in the face of market pressures, never lose their curiosity about the world around them, and are always prepared to rise to the next big challenge that is just around the corner are the real masters of their profession.

www.ingramcontent.com/pod-product-compliance
Lightning Source LLC
Chambersburg PA
CBHW072000210526
45479CB00003B/1016